PREHISTORIC
MARINE REPTILES

Prehistoric Marine Reptiles

SEA MONSTERS DURING THE AGE OF DINOSAURS

JUDY A. MASSARE, Ph.D.

FRANKLIN WATTS
New York ▪ London ▪ Toronto ▪ Sydney
1991

FOR ESHAN

Original art courtesy of Gautam Mitra:
pp. 15, 25, 31, 33, 36, 44, 53;

Photographs and diagrams courtesy of the author.

Library of Congress Cataloging-in-Publication Data

Massare, Judy A.
Prehistoric marine reptiles: sea monsters during the age of
dinosaurs / Judy A. Massare.
p.   cm.
Includes bibliographical references and index.
Summary: Describes the prehistoric reptiles which
inhabited the waters at the time that the dinosaurs
were ruling on land.
ISBN 0-531-11022-2
1. Reptiles, Fossil—Juvenile literature. 2. Paleontology-
Mesozoic Juvenile literature. [1. Reptiles, Fossil.
2. Prehistoric animals.] I. Title.
QE861.M37 1991
14567.9—dc20   91-17057   CIP   AC

CONTENTS

PREHISTORIC MARINE REPTILES

CHAPTER 1

Introducing the Mesozoic Sea Monsters

The Mesozoic Era started 245 million years ago and ended 65 million years ago. During that time, reptiles ruled the land and oceans. For this reason, the Mesozoic Era is often called the Age of Reptiles. While dinosaurs dominated *habitats* on land, several other kinds of reptiles ruled the oceans. These ocean-going reptiles are called *marine* reptiles.

The Mesozoic marine reptiles included ichthyosaurs, plesiosaurs, nothosaurs, placodonts, sea turtles, mosasaurs, and two kinds of marine crocodiles—teleosaurs and geosaurs. Not all of these reptiles lived at the same time. Certain kinds were common during specific periods of the Mesozoic Era.

The Mesozoic Era is divided into three periods. The Triassic Period was from 245 to 208 million years ago. The Jurassic Period was from 208 to 145 million years ago. The Cretaceous Period was from 145 to 65 million years ago. Ichthyosaurs, placodonts, and nothosaurs lived in the Triassic oceans. Ichthyosaurs, plesiosaurs, geosaurs, and teleosaurs shared the seas during the Jurassic and earliest part of the Cretaceous periods. Mosasaurs, plesiosaurs, and sea turtles dominated during the later part of the Cretaceous Period. By the end of the Cretaceous Period, all of the marine reptiles, except the turtles, had become *extinct.* Only sea turtles still live in the oceans today, although living sea turtles are different from their Mesozoic ancestors.

The chart shows the way *paleontologists* (scientists who study fossils) summarize information about when animals lived. The time periods are listed from the oldest, at the bottom of the chart, to the youngest, or most recent, at the top of the chart. There is one vertical bar for each kind of marine reptile. Each bar begins at the level representing the time that the group first appeared on earth. The bars end at the time that the group became extinct. If you pick a particular time in the Mesozoic Era, by reading across the chart you can see which kinds of marine reptiles were living at the same time.

Many kinds of marine reptiles lived at the same time as dinosaurs, but they were not dinosaurs, even though some of them were just as large. Dinosaurs are distinguished from other reptiles by the arrangement of bones in their skull, by the structure of their hip, and by the shape of their ankle bones. None of the marine reptiles had any of these features, and so were not closely related to dinosaurs. In fact, the different kinds of marine reptiles did not have many features in common, indicating that they were not closely related to each other, either.

The dinosaurs all share certain skeletal characteristics because these traits were inherited from

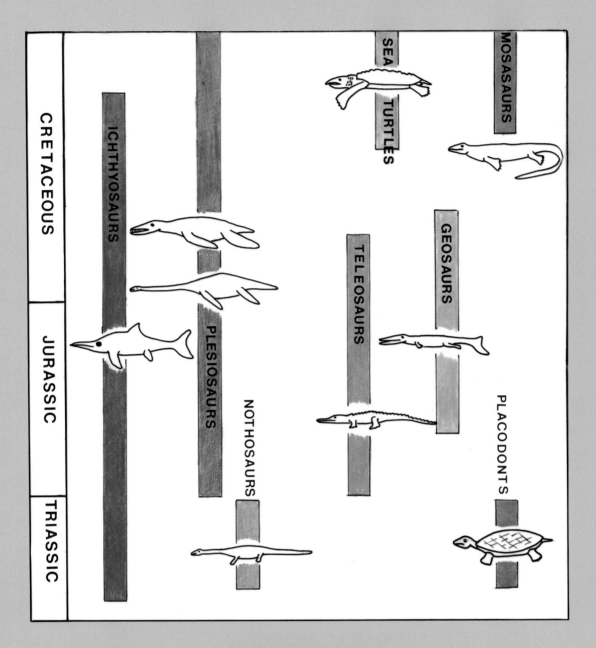

*The geologic time ranges for
the major marine reptile groups
of the Mesozoic Era*

the same ancestor. The many kinds of dinosaurs can therefore be thought of as "cousins" to one another. The different kinds of marine reptiles have few skeletal characteristics in common except for those found in all reptiles. Each main group of marine reptiles probably evolved from a different ancestor, and so the groups are not closely related to either one another or to the dinosaurs.

The marine reptiles were similar to each other in the way they lived. They probably had habits much like those of living marine mammals, namely dolphins, whales, seals, and sea lions. Marine reptiles, like marine mammals of today, were the largest *predators* in the oceans. Most of them were active swimmers and caught other swimming animals for their *prey*. The reptiles had many kinds of marine life from which to choose—fish, squidlike animals, ammonoids, and even other marine reptiles. The marine reptiles, like most living reptiles, could not chew their food. Instead, they probably used their teeth to catch prey and then swallowed it whole. If you have ever watched seals or dolphins being fed at a zoo or aquarium, you know that this is exactly how they eat fish. The marine reptiles must have eaten animals much smaller than themselves. The size of their prey was probably determined by how large an animal they could swallow whole. Paleontologists can estimate the size of the prey eaten by a particular marine reptile by measuring the width of the back of the predator's skull.

Like today's marine mammals, all of the marine reptiles needed to breathe air to live, even though they spent most of their time in the water. Marine reptiles were probably cold-blooded, as are all living reptiles. Because reptiles are cold-blooded, they need less oxygen for their size than mammals do. So marine reptiles could probably dive and remain under water for long periods of time, possibly even an hour or more! But eventually they had to return to the surface to breathe.

All of the marine reptiles were adapted in some way for swimming. Some were faster swimmers than others, and they did not all swim in the same way. Mosasaurs, geosaurs, and teleosaurs swam by undulating their long, flexible bodies and long, broad tails in the same way that living crocodiles swim. The plesiosaurs swam using their two pairs of flat, tapered legs as wings to fly underwater like penguins do. Ichthyosaurs swam by moving their crescent-shaped tail fins back and forth, similar to the way fish swim.

CHAPTER 2

Ichthyosaurs
THE FISH-LIZARDS

Ichthyosaurs were the first of the marine reptiles to appear on earth. The word *ichthyosaur* means "fish (ichthyo-) lizard (-saur)." The oldest ichthyosaur fossils are from the early part of the Triassic Period. They appeared on earth about 15 to 20 million years before the first dinosaurs. They have no close living relatives, so everything we know about ichthyosaurs comes from fossils.

Ichthyosaurs came in many shapes and sizes. One of the smallest ichthyosaurs, named *Mixosaurus*, was only about 3 feet (1 m) long when fully grown. The largest ichthyosaur, *Shonisaurus*, was over 40 feet (13 m) long. That's about the length of a school bus. *Shonisaurus* was the largest animal on earth during the last part of the Triassic Period. Most ichthyosaurs, however, were about 7 to 10 feet (2 to 3 m) long, about the size of living dolphins. The ichthyosaur ancestors were probably lizardlike animals that lived along the shore, but ichthyosaurs show few similarities with *terrestrial* reptiles. Ichthyosaurs evolved many *adaptations* for living in water, so they resemble other aquatic animals, such as fish and dolphins, more than they resemble lizards.

A Stenopterygius *group and an*
Eurhinosaurus *search for food in*
the Jurassic seas of Europe.

Instead of the long, narrow body that lizards have, most ichthyosaurs had a body shape that gave them a streamlined look. The bony connection between the hips and backbone that helps support animals while standing or walking was absent in ichthyosaurs. This means that their legs could probably not support them on land. Furthermore, instead of long legs with five separated toes, the legs of ichthyosaurs had short, flat bones that interlocked to form a stiff flipper. The tail of an ichthyosaur was not straight as in lizards, but was sharply bent downward toward the end. The slope supported the lower lobe of a crescent-shaped, vertically oriented tail fin. Many ichthyosaurs also had a dorsal fin, a fin on their backs similar to that found on many sharks and fish.

Ichthyosaurs swam by moving their tail back and forth, the way most fish swim. Their flippers were most likely used for steering. The dorsal fin helped to stabilize them at high speeds by preventing them from rolling from side to side. Their streamlined bodies made them very efficient swimmers. Like today's dolphins, ichythyosaurs could probably swim fairly fast and for long distances without getting tired.

Most reptiles lay eggs to reproduce. Unlike fish or amphibian eggs, these have to be laid on land because they need oxygen from the air to develop. With so many adaptations for living in the water, how could ichthyosaurs return to land to lay eggs? The surprising answer was found in some fossils from England and southern Germany, first discovered in the 1840s. These fossils preserved the tiny skeletons

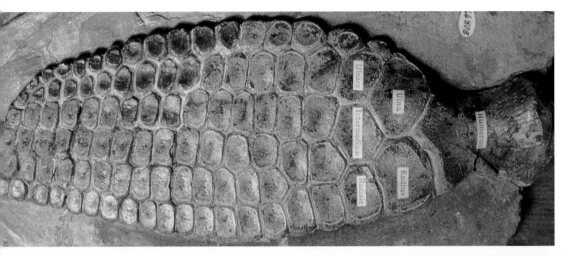

Top: Front limb of an ichthyosaur.
Note the many short, wide finger
bones that fit together to
form a stiff paddle.
Bottom: Fossil of a young ichthyosaur
that preserves the body outline,
showing a dorsal fin and
a crescent-shaped tail

ICHTHYOSAURUS COMMUNIS, Conybeare.
LOWER LIAS   LYME REGIS, DORSETSHIRE.

Skull (about .5 meters long)
of Ichthyosaurus, a Jurassic
ichthyosaur from Europe. It had
blunt teeth used to grasp prey
with a fairly hard exterior,
as well as softer prey.

of unborn (*embryo*) ichythyosaurs within the skeleton of adult ichythyosaurs. This led paleontologists to conclude that ichthyosaurs gave birth to live young, rather than laying eggs as most reptiles do. This meant that they never had to return to land to lay eggs. Ichthyosaurs probably traveled to shallow coastal waters to give birth, as do many species of living whales. Since their first discovery, quite a few specimens of ichthyosaur embryos have been found within the skeleton of the mother, most of them from southern Germany.

All ichthyosaurs probably preyed upon small swimming animals. Their long, fairly narrow snout and jaws supported long rows of teeth that lined the mouth. The narrow snout reduced the resistance of the water as the jaws opened and snapped shut to catch prey. Ichthyosaurs did not all eat exactly the same thing. The shape of the teeth has been used by paleontologists to make guesses as to what kinds of organisms each kind of ichthyosaur ate. Some ichthyosaurs had slender pointed teeth that were probably used to pierce soft prey, such as small fish and squid. Others had broad teeth with rounded rather than pointed ends. These teeth were probably used to grasp and crush prey with a fairly hard exterior, such as armored fish with thick, bony scales. Still other ichthyosaurs had teeth with blade-like ridges on each side. They probably were used to catch large fish and other marine reptiles. This kind of tooth is found in some of the largest ichthyosaurs.

Ichthyosaurs became extinct about 85 million years ago, toward the end of the Cretaceous Period.

CHAPTER 3

Life in the Triassic Oceans

The oceans of the Triassic Period were different in size and shape from today's oceans. During the Triassic, the continents were all united into one large supercontinent geologists call Pangea. The shallow seas surrounding Pangea were the home of the first marine reptiles.

Our best picture of Triassic reptiles comes from southern Switzerland and northern Italy. During the middle part of the Triassic, this area was covered by a shallow sea. The soft black mud on the seafloor was just right for preserving the skeletons of marine animals that had died and settled to the bottom. The black shales that formed from the mud contain many fossils that tell us what kinds of marine reptiles lived in the Triassic seas: ichthyosaurs, placodonts, and nothosaurs.

Nothosaurs ranged in size from small animals only 12 inches (30 cm) long to giants such as *Ceresiosaurus* and *Nothosaurus*, which were over 13 feet (5.4 m) long. Nothosaurs looked like very long-necked lizards. Even though their necks, bodies, and tails were long, their legs were fairly short. Nothosaurs

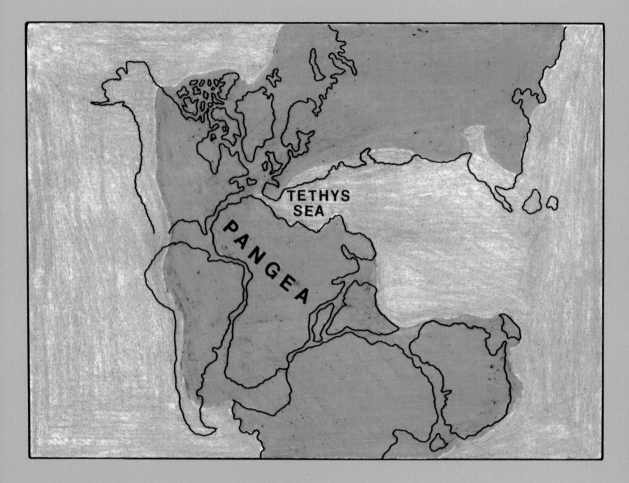

Map showing the distribution
of land and oceans during the
middle of the Triassic Period.
Present-day continents are
outlined in black.

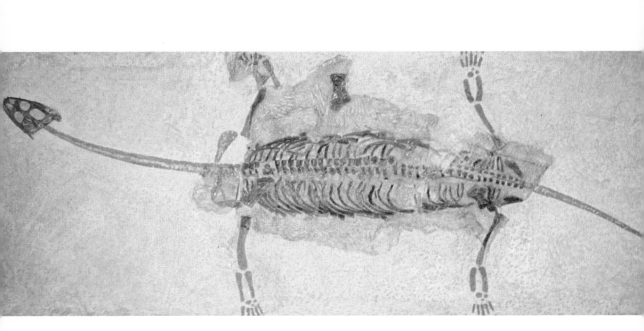

Flattened skeleton of the large nothosaur
Simosaurus (approximately 2.25 meters long).
The rear half of the tail is missing.

had few adaptations for swimming, except for long toes that were probably webbed like the feet of ducks. Most likely they could paddle around slowly, using their webbed feet. They probably swam faster by undulating their long bodies and tails in the same way that living crocodiles do. At least some nothosaurs might have been able to walk on land, and probably spent time basking in the sun on shore. They hunted for food in the shallow coastal waters. Even the largest nothosaurs had small heads, just over a foot (40 cm) long, so they could not have eaten very large animals. They probably fed on small fish and other soft prey, which they caught with their slender, pointed teeth.

Sharing the shallow coastal waters with nothosaurs were the placodonts, probably the most unusual of all the marine reptiles. *Placodus*, one of the first placodonts to appear, was a large, heavy reptile 5 feet (1.5 m) long. Along its spine was a row of thick, bony plates that probably served as armor to protect its spinal cord from attack by predators. Some placodonts, such as *Placochelys*, were completely covered with bony armor that formed a shell, like a turtle's, over the whole body. Placodonts were not closely related to turtles and became extinct before turtles evolved. Placodonts were probably slow swimmers that paddled along the seafloor in search of clams and other shellfish. The curved front teeth of placodonts were angled outward. They were probably used to pluck clams from the seafloor. Their heavy skulls had large muscles for closing the jaws. On the side and roof of their mouth were broad, flat teeth that were used to crush hard shells.

The largest and most widespread of the Triassic predators were the ichthyosaurs. Ichthyosaurs shared the coastal waters with placodonts and nothosaurs. Some ichthyosaurs, especially the largest ones, also inhabited deeper water farther offshore.

Triassic ichthyosaurs showed more advanced adaptations for living in water than either the nothosaurs or placodonts. They did not have as many adaptations for fast, continuous swimming as did later Jurassic and Cretaceous ichythosaurs. Most Triassic ichthyosaurs had long bodies that were not very streamlined. Their tails lacked the down-turned bend and tail fin found in later ichthyosaurs. Instead, the tail was nearly straight and fairly broad. Because of

Skeleton of the placodont Placodus, *about 1.5 meters long, from the Triassic of Europe*

this, many Triassic ichthyosaurs probably swam more like crocodiles than like fish. They were adapted for short bursts of speed rather than long-distance chases. They could chase slow prey, but probably waited for prey to swim by and caught them with a quick lunge.

Some Triassic ichthyosaurs had more than one kind of tooth in their jaws (*Mixosaurus*, for example). The front teeth were slender and pointed, and the back teeth were flat and blunt. This arrangement probably allowed them to catch soft prey with their front teeth and crush hard prey with their back

*A placodont feeds on clams as the small
ichthyosaur* Mixosaurus *swims in the
distance. Note that* Mixosaurus *lacks
the crescent-shaped tail present on
Jurassic and Cretaceous ichthyosaurs.*

teeth. This is very unusual because most marine reptiles had only one kind of tooth.

Placodonts and nothosaurs became extinct by the
end of the Triassic Period. The ichthyosaurs, however, survived into Jurassic time, when they shared
the oceans with entirely different kinds of reptiles.

CHAPTER 4

Plesiosaurs

Plesiosaurs first appeared at the beginning of the Jurassic Period. They are unique among marine reptiles because they swam by using only their legs rather than their tails. Their long, tapered legs looked like wings. Their leg bones were flattened and probably could not move at the knee or ankle. Their toes were extremely long; some were made up of a dozen or more individual bones. By comparison, we have only three bones in each finger or toe! Paleontologists of the 1800s thought that plesiosaurs used their legs like oars to row along the surface of the water. However, most paleontologists now think that the legs were used as wings, so that plesiosaurs flew through the water much the way penguins do today. Plesiosaur tails were fairly short, and were probably used to help steer, like the rudder of a boat.

There were two kinds of plesiosaurs: long-necked plesiosaurs with very small heads, and short-necked plesiosaurs with large heads. The second kind are often called pliosaurs. The two kinds were probably quite different in the way that they attacked prey and in the type of food they ate.

The long-necked plesiosaurs varied in the relative length of the neck. The Jurassic plesiosaur *Muraneosaurus*, for example, reached a length of about 20 feet (6 m), of which 8 feet (2.5 m) was the neck alone!

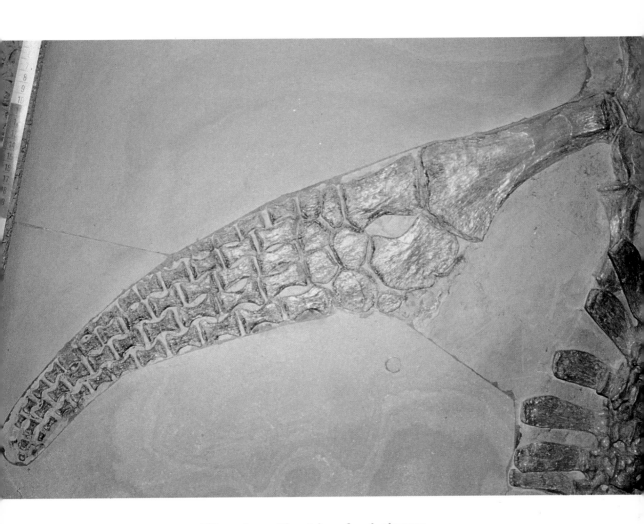

Wing-shaped front leg of a plesiosaur,
Brachypterygius, from the Jurassic Period

The largest-known plesiosaurs lived during the Cretaceous Period. They also had the longest necks, made up of as many as sixty or seventy *vertebrae*. *Thalassomedon*, found in Colorado, was 40 feet (12 m) long, but over 20 feet of that (6.5 m) was the neck. *Elasmosaurus*, found in Kansas, had a neck 23 feet (7 m) long, and a total length of 41 feet (12.5 m).

Skeleton of the long-necked plesiosaur Alzadasaurus, from the Cretaceous Period of North America

The long necks of plesiosaurs gave them a very unstreamlined shape. They probably were not fast swimmers, at least as compared to pliosaurs and ichthyosaurs of the same size. The long neck may have also created some problems for them in maneuvering or maintaining their balance in the water. Many plesiosaurs have been found with numerous smooth, polished pebbles in the stomach region. These stomach stones are called *gastroliths*. Plesiosaurs probably swallowed them to add extra weight to stabilize themselves in the water.

The long-necked plesiosaurs had a very small head. Even the longest plesiosaur had a head less than 2 feet (60 cm) long. Long-necked plesiosaurs must have therefore eaten relatively small prey. Their long, slender, pointed teeth may have formed a sieve for trapping fish. Or they may have used their teeth to pierce the soft skins of small fish and squid. Most long-necked plesiosaurs had eyes that faced upward and forward, suggesting that they approached prey from below. They may have caught food by swimming under schools of small fish, then raising their head into the center of the school and snapping up mouthfuls of fish. The long neck would permit a surprise attack because the small head would reach the school before the bulkier body could be detected by the fish.

Pliosaurs were different sorts of predators. Most were 10 to 15 feet (3-4 m) long, but some reached huge sizes. Pliosaurs had much larger heads than the long-necked plesiosaurs, and so could eat larger prey. The largest known pliosaur, *Kronosaurus*, lived in Australia during the Cretaceous Period. It was 43 feet (13 m) long, or as long as the dinosaur *Tyrannosaurus rex*. Its head was 8 feet (2.5 m) long. It could have easily swallowed a small ichthyosaur in a single gulp!

Because of their relatively short necks, pliosaurs had a much more compact shape than the long-

*Above: Note the long slender teeth
in this skull of Brachypterygius
[about 12 centimeters long],
a long-necked plesiosaur from
the Jurassic Period of Germany.*

*Facing page: A hungry Cretaceous plesiosaur
surprises a school of fish from below.*

necked plesiosaurs. Their legs were also much larger. They were probably faster swimmers than long-necked plesiosaurs of the same size. Like the ichthyosaurs, they could probably swim long distances in search of prey. Their eyes faced forward and somewhat to the side, suggesting that they caught prey from behind, probably after a chase. The largest pliosaurs had big, strong teeth with numerous blade-like ridges running from the base of the tooth to the tip. These teeth were designed for cutting and tearing flesh. They could probably catch large fish or even other marine reptiles. The smaller pliosaurs had slender, curved, pointed teeth, probably for catching fish or squid.

Skeleton of Peloneustes (about 4 meters long), a Jurassic pliosaur from England

The pliosaur Peloneustes *attacks a fish.*

How did plesiosaurs manage to move on land to lay eggs? Oceangoing animals rely on the water to help support their weight. On land, their muscles are often not strong enough to support them. This is the problem that whales face when they are washed up on beaches. Plesiosaurs had fairly stiff backs and riblike bones called *gastralia* that protected their bellies. This combination may have kept the body from collapsing under its own weight when the plesiosaur was on land. Plesiosaurs may have been able to move around the way seals do. Would the long-necked plesiosaurs have been strong enough to hold up their neck on land without the help of water for support? No one knows for sure. No fossils of plesiosaur eggs or baby plesiosaurs have ever been found. Whether they laid eggs on land or gave birth to live young as the ichthyosaurs did will remain a mystery until someone—maybe even you—discovers fossil eggs or embryos and learns the answer.

Plesiosaurs became extinct at the end of the Cretaceous Period. They have no living relatives, unless you believe in the Loch Ness monster!

CHAPTER 5

Marine Crocodiles

GEOSAURS AND TELEOSAURS

During the Jurassic Period and the earliest part of the Cretaceous Period, there were two kinds of oceangoing crocodiles—the teleosaurs and the geosaurs. The largest of these animals reached a length of about 16 and a half feet (5 m), but most were moderate-sized, 6 to 10 feet (2-3 m) in length. One difference between the marine crocodiles and the crocodiles living along the shore was that the marine crocodiles had very long, narrow snouts. This was an adaptation for having to open and close their jaws in water. The narrow shape reduced the resistance of the water against their jaws and required less muscle power to snap them shut quickly under water than would be needed by a wide snout.

The marine crocodiles swam the way living crocodiles do, by undulating their long bodies and tails. Their legs were held flat against the body while swimming. Often the tail was flattened side to side to provide a broader surface for pushing against the water. This method of swimming is not very good for fast, long-distance swimming, but is well suited for

A Jurassic geosaur surprises a fish.

rapid acceleration and sudden bursts of speed. The marine crocodiles probably lay motionless in the water or on the seafloor, waiting for prey to swim by. They would then try to catch it with a quick lunge, rather than chasing it for a long distance.

What did marine crocodiles eat? As with the other marine reptiles, the food probably depended on the skull size and on the kind of teeth that a particular *species* had. Some of the small crocodiles, such as *Pegalosaurus*, had slender, pointed teeth that were probably used to catch small fish. Others, like *Dakosaurus*, one of the largest geosaurs, had large, strong teeth with serrated ridges in front and back, like steak knives. These teeth were well suited for killing large fish and other marine reptiles. As a group, the marine crocodiles had the same variety of food in their diets as any of the other groups of marine reptiles. The big difference was in the way in which they caught their prey—by *ambush* (surprise attack)—rather than by *pursuit* (long-distance chase).

Both geosaurs and teleosaurs were marine crocodiles, but they were different from each other. The teleosaurs were covered with bony plates, located under the scaly skin of their back and belly. These plates, called *scutes*, could move in relation to one another. They provided a flexible suit of armor for protection against large predators such as the giant pliosaurs. Most species of living and fossil crocodiles have similar bony armor. The geosaurs, however, completely lacked armor. This may have made their body lighter than that of the teleosaurs. Perhaps geosaurs were faster swimmers than the teleosaurs.

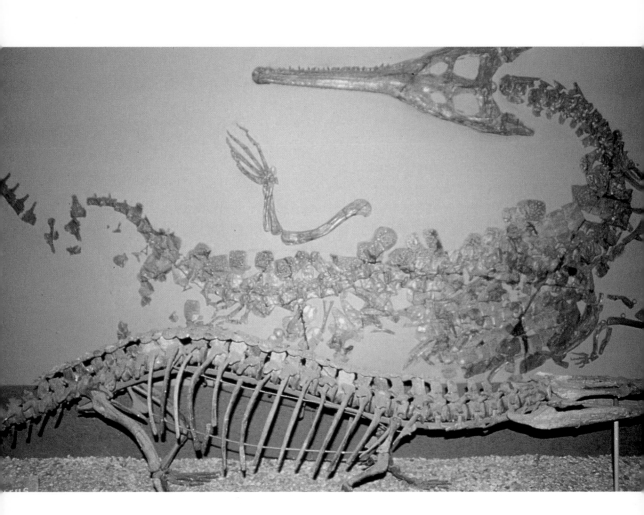

This skeleton of the teleosaur Stenosaurus shows the many bony plates that made up the armor covering its body. Notice the very long, slender snout that is typical of marine crocodiles. Skull length is approximately 75 centimeters.

Geosaurs also had unusual tails. Most crocodiles, including teleosaurs, have long, straight tails. Geosaurs had a downturned bend toward the end of the tail. The curve probably supported some kind of small tail fin, although not as big as the one on the ichthyosaurs. The front legs of geosaurs were also unusual. They were very short, less than half the size of the back legs. And they were shaped more like broad paddles than like terrestrial crocodile legs. Geosaurs may have used their front legs to help steer while tucking their longer back legs against their body as they swam.

Like living crocodiles, geosaurs and teleosaurs probably had to return to land to lay eggs. The short front legs and downturned tail of the geosaurs must have made walking on land difficult. The teleosaurs

The white outline shows the probable shape of the tail of the Jurassic geosaur Metriorhynchus, about 2.5 meters long. Notice how much larger the hind legs are than the front legs.

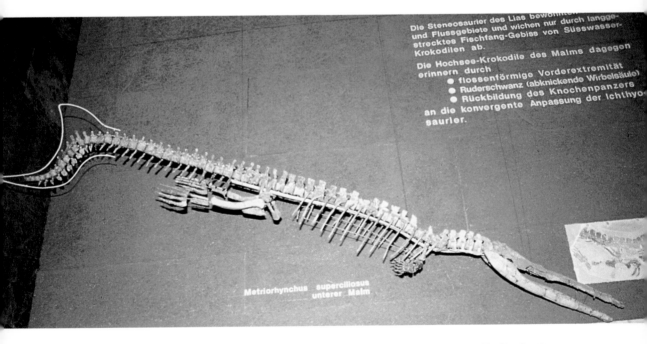

Die Steneosaurier des Lias bewohnten und Flussgebiete und wichen nur durch langgestrecktes Fischfang-Gebiss von Süsswasser-Krokodilen ab.

Die Hochsee-Krokodile des Malms dagegen erinnern durch
● flossenförmige Vorderextremität
● Ruderschwanz (abknickende Wirbelsäule)
● Rückbildung des Knochenpanzers
an die konvergente Anpassung der Ichthyosaurier.

Metriorhynchus superciliosus
unterer Malm

and geosaurs may have come ashore on beaches and dug nests in the sand with their back legs. After depositing the eggs, they may have covered them with warm sand to let them incubate. Living crocodiles often stay near their nest to guard the eggs until they hatch. Did the marine crocodiles guard their eggs as well? Perhaps they did, dividing their time between watching the nest and hunting for food in the shallow waters along the shore.

The marine crocodiles were most abundant during the last half of the Jurassic Period. Both kinds, geosaurs and teleosaurs, became extinct in the early part of the Cretaceous Period. Their "cousins" on land still survive today.

CHAPTER 6

Life in the Jurassic Oceans

During the Jurassic Period, the supercontinent Pangea began to break apart. A northern supercontinent, called Laurasia, was made up of the present-day continents of North America, Europe, and Asia. A southern supercontinent, called Gondwanaland, was made up of South America, Africa, Australia, Antarctica, and India. An ocean called the Tethys Sea separated eastern Laurasia from Gondwanaland.

In what is today southern Germany, a sheltered area of the Tethys Sea (perhaps a deep lagoon or bay) attracted many kinds of marine reptiles. The bodies of those that died settled to the seafloor and sank into a dense black mud. Today, the black shales that formed from that mud contain spectacular fossils of fish, ichthyosaurs, plesiosaurs, and teleosaurs. They are found in quarries in the town of Holzmaden, Germany, where they have been collected by paleontologists for over one hundred years. These fossils show us some of the animals that lived in the Tethys Sea. They have provided a great deal of information on life in the oceans during the early part of the Jurassic Period.

Map showing the distribution
of land and oceans during the middle
of the Jurassic Period. Present-day
continents are outlined in black.

The most diverse and abundant of all the marine reptiles were the ichthyosaurs. Most common was *Stenopterygius*, a medium-sized ichthyosaur that ate squidlike animals. In some specimens, the hook-like barbs from "squid" tentacles are preserved within the skeleton of the ichthyosaur in the area where the stomach would be in a living animal. This kind of evidence is rarely preserved in fossils, and emphasizes how unusual the Holzmaden fossils are. The giant ichthyosaur, *Leptopterygius*, reached a length of 26 feet (8 m). Fortunately for the smaller ichthyosaurs, there were not very many of them. *Leptopterygius* was the "killer whale" of the early Jurassic, feeding on smaller ichthyosaurs, large fish, and probably anything else it could find. The oddest of the ichthyosaurs was *Eurhinosaurus*. It had an extremely long, narrow snout with many slender, pointed teeth. But the lower jaw was only one-third the length of the snout! How did it eat? It may have used its snout the way a swordfish does, slashing at schools of small fish and killing some of them, which it would later scoop up and swallow. But no one knows for certain why the lower jaw was so short.

Besides many species of ichthyosaurs, there were a few plesiosaurs and pliosaurs. The plesiosaurs were about 10 feet (3 m) long. The pliosaurs were only slightly larger, almost 12 feet (3.6 m) long. Both groups probably preyed upon small fish or squid— with the plesiosaurs catching their prey by a surprise attack from below, and the pliosaurs chasing them from behind over some distance. And they all tried to avoid the largest ichthyosaurs! A few kinds

*Two large pliosaurs, Liopleurodons, chase a
smaller plesiosaur, Cryptoclidus.*

of teleosaurs were also present, but they were not
very abundant. They may have lurked along the seafloor, darting upward to catch prey that swam too
close.

Another picture of life in the Jurassic oceans
comes from England. During the later part of the
Jurassic, a shallow sea covered much of central and

southern England. The many marine reptile skeletons discovered there show us that sea life during the last half of the Jurassic was different than in earlier times. There were fewer kinds of ichthyosaurs, but more kinds of plesiosaurs and crocodiles. The common ichthyosaur was *Ophthalmosaurus*, notable for its very large eyes. Paleontologists have suggested that it hunted for squid at night, or maybe hunted in very deep water that got very little sunlight. Large pliosaurs took the place of the large ichthyosaurs as the biggest and fastest predators in the oceans. Some of these pliosaurs had skulls that were over 6 feet (2 m) long. They could have easily eaten any of the other marine reptiles. Smaller pliosaurs such as *Peloneustes* were also present. They probably ate fish and squid. Long-necked plesiosaurs were more abundant than in earlier times. They fed on small fish. Both geosaurs and teleosaurs were also common. Their ambush method of capturing prey meant that they did not have to compete with the faster ichthyosaurs and pliosaurs for food. This very *diverse* community of marine reptiles probably continued into the earliest part of the Cretaceous Period.

CHAPTER 7

Mosasaurs

THE LAST OF
THE SEA MONSTERS

The mosasaurs were the last of the prehistoric marine reptiles to appear. They lived during the late Cretaceous Period, after the geosaurs, teleosaurs, and most of the ichthyosaurs had become extinct. Mosasaurs were giant ocean-going lizards with elongated bodies and very long tails. They are closely related to today's monitor lizards. The largest mosasaurs reached lengths of 33 feet (10 m) or more.

Like today's crocodiles, mosasaurs probably swam by undulating their long bodies and tails. Their short legs had long, spreading toes that were probably webbed. They used their legs for maneuvering and changing direction. Their legs were much too short to support them on land. As did the other long-bodied predators, mosasaurs probably caught their food by ambush rather than by chasing prey over long distances.

Most mosasaurs had large, strong teeth with sharp ridges in the back and front. With this kind of dental arsenal, they did not have to be too particular about what they ate. The smaller mosasaur species probably ate squid and fish. The large ones, such as

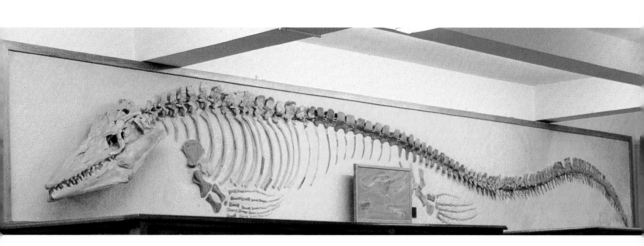

*Skeleton of the large mosasaur, Tylosaurus,
[over 4 meters long], from the
Cretaceous Period of Kansas*

Tylosaurus and *Mosasaurus*, could eat almost anything except clams and other thick-shelled ammonoids. Mosasaurs had a varied diet. A mosasaur skeleton from South Dakota preserved the remains of *aquatic* birds, pterosaurs, fish, and another mosasaur in between the ribs where the stomach must have been. The most unusual mosasaur was *Globidens.* It had typical mosasaur teeth in front, but it had blunt, acorn-shaped teeth in the back. *Globidens* almost certainly ate clams and ammonoids, crushing their shells with its massive back teeth.

An unusual feature of mosasaurs is that the middle of their lower jaw was hinged. This joint allowed them to open their mouths so wide that they could swallow large prey. Mosasaurs had curved, pointed teeth on the roof of their mouth. They used these teeth to help pull in large prey to be swallowed.

Skull of **Platecarpus,** *a mosasaur from the Cretaceous Period of Kansas. Note the hinge in the jaw right below the eye.*

Paleontologists are presently debating how mosasaurs reproduced. It is difficult to imagine them moving on land to lay eggs. Their legs were much too short to support them. They may have snaked along on their bellies, but this too is unlikely. Mosasaurs had very short ribs. Most of their rib cage was made of cartilage, which is much softer than bone. (Your ears are made of cartilage.) The mosasaur rib cage could not have supported the animal on land. The chest would have collapsed under the weight of the animal, thereby preventing it from breathing. These and other features suggest that mosasaurs may have given birth to live young, as did ichthyosaurs, rather than laying eggs. No mosasaur eggs or embryos have ever been found. Until some firm evidence is discovered, the debate will continue.

Mosasaurs became extinct at the end of the Cretaceous Period. Their close relatives, the monitor lizards, are still living today in warm, tropical environments.

CHAPTER 8

Life in the Cretaceous Oceans

The two supercontinents, Laurasia and Gondwanaland, continued to break apart throughout the Cretaceous Period. South America and Africa spread apart as the southern Atlantic Ocean widened. Antarctica, Australia, and India separated, and had moved near their present positions by the end of the Cretaceous Period. North America and Europe slowly spread apart as the northern Atlantic Ocean continued to widen. The movement of the continents was slow, only a few centimeters per year, but over millions of years this produced large changes. Continent positions affect the climate on land and the circulation patterns of the oceans. So environments were changing throughout the Cretaceous, especially toward the end.

Little is known about marine reptiles in the early part of the Cretaceous. Most of our information on the Triassic and Jurassic comes from a few locations where many well-preserved fossils have been discovered. There is no such locality known dating from the Early Cretaceous age. Early Cretaceous marine reptile fossils are fragmentary and scattered. A few facts are known. Both geosaurs and teleosaurs be-

ASIAMERICA

EURAMERICA

ASIAMERICA

ASIAMERICA

Map showing the distribution
of land and oceans during the middle
of the Cretaceous Period. Present-day
continents are outlined in black.

came extinct in the early part of the Cretaceous. Ichthyosaurs were rare. Long-necked plesiosaurs (called elasmosaurs in the Cretaceous) and large pliosaurs were still around, but not as diverse or abundant as they were in the late Jurassic oceans.

The picture is quite different in the Late Cretaceous oceans. Sea level was unusually high because there were no polar ice caps. Inland seas covered the interiors of many continents. North America was divided by a seaway that covered the central part of the continent from the Arctic Ocean to the Gulf of Mexico. This seaway was home to many marine reptiles. The Cretaceous black shales and chalks of Kansas, South Dakota, eastern Wyoming, and Alabama are known for their marine reptile fossils. These fossils show that mosasaurs were the most common reptile in the interior seaway. There were many species, but they all were similar in their method of swimming and in the kind of teeth they had. They were unspecialized predators, eating almost anything of the appropriate size. They shared the sea with elasmosaurs, small pliosaurs, and sea turtles.

The elasmosaurs, like other long-necked plesiosaurs, probably ate small fish and squid. They probably attacked schools of fish from below. Most elasmosaurs had extremely long necks, which may have been flexible enough to dart out at fast-moving prey. The pliosaurs were small and chased down fish and squid for their food. The sea turtles may have been scavengers. Some of them were huge, with shells 8 feet (2.5 m) in diameter. Turtles were most abundant in the southern part of the seaway. Large

*An **Elasmosaurus** tries to defend itself
from a larger mosasaur,* Mosasaurus, *in
the shallow inland sea of North America.*

fish and large sharks were also common in the late
Cretaceous. In fact, fossils of large fish are more
abundant than those of reptiles.

By the end of the Cretaceous Period, the mosasaurs, pliosaurs, and elasmosaurs had become ex-

tinct. Why? We will probably never know for sure. The inland seas dried up toward the end of the Cretaceous Period. This may have eliminated important habitats for the marine reptiles. A change in the ocean circulation caused by the changing position of the continents may have added to the problem. The remaining areas may have been too cold for the marine reptiles or for the animals that they depended on for food. The marine reptiles seem to have disappeared several million years before the last of the dinosaurs. The extinction of the dinosaurs and the marine reptiles may not have been caused by the same factors.

Where to See Marine Reptile Fossils

Many museums in the United States and Canada have marine reptile fossils on display. The following have some of the largest exhibits:

Academy of Natural Science, Philadelphia, Pennsylvania

Berlin-Ichthyosaur State Park, Austin (actually closer to Gabbs), Nevada

National Museum of Natural History, Smithsonian Institution, Washington, D.C.

Natural History Museum, University of Kansas, Lawrence, Kansas

Sternberg Memorial Museum, Ft. Hays State College, Hays, Kansas

Tyrrell Museum, Drumheller, Alberta

Other museums with some marine reptiles on display include:

American Museum of Natural History,
New York, New York

Natural History Museum, Carnegie Institute,
Pittsburgh, Pennsylvania

Denver Museum of Natural History,
Denver, Colorado

Geology Museum, University of Colorado,
Boulder, Colorado

Geology Museum, University of Nevada,
Las Vegas, Nevada

Geology Museum, University of Wyoming,
Laramie, Wyoming

Geology Museum, South Dakota School of
Mines and Technology, Rapid City, South
Dakota

Royal Ontario Museum, Toronto, Ontario

State Museum of Natural History, Lincoln,
Nebraska

This list does not include every museum with marine reptile fossils. Check the museum nearest you. You might be surprised to find a marine reptile fossil in their exhibits.

Adaptation—a trait acquired through evolution that enables an animal to do something better than its ancestors.

Ambush predator—a predator that lies hidden, waiting for prey to come near, and catches it with a quick burst of speed.

Aquatic—living in water.

Diverse—having many different kinds.

Diversity—the number of different kinds of plants or animals.

Embryo—an unborn animal either still inside an egg or the body of its mother.

Extinct—no longer existing.

Gastralia—riblike bones that supported the belly of plesiosaurs.

Gastroliths—stomach stones; rounded, smooth stones found where the stomach would have been in long-necked plesiosaurs.

Habitat—the place or type of place where an animal (or plant) usually lives.

Marine—relating to the oceans.

Paleontologist—a scientist who studies fossils to determine what extinct animals looked like and how they lived.

Predator—an animal that lives by catching and eating other animals.

Prey—animals caught for food by a predator.

Pursuit predator—a predator that actively searches for prey and chases it down, sometimes over considerable distances.

Scutes—bony plates found just below the skin of crocodiles.

Species—a particular kind of animal or plant.

Terrestrial—living on land.

Vertebra—one of a series of disklike or cylindrical bones that makes up the backbone.

Vertebrae—more than one vertebra.

Benton, Michael. *The Giant Book of Dinosaurs.* New York: Gallery Books, 1988.

____ . *On the Trail of the Dinosaurs.* New York: Crescent Books, 1989.

Dixon, Dougal; Barry Cox; R.J.G. Savage; and Brian Gardiner. *The Macmillan Illustrated Encyclopedia of Dinosaurs and Prehistoric Animals.* New York: American Museum of Natural History, 1988.

Norman, David. *An Illustrated Encyclopedia of Dinosaurs.* New York: Crescent Books, 1985.

____ . *When Dinosaurs Ruled the Earth.* New York: Dorset Press, 1990.

ABOUT THE AUTHOR

Judy Massare has a Ph.D. in paleontology from the Johns Hopkins University. Her research on the ecology and evolution of extinct marine reptiles has resulted in the publication of several articles in professional journals. She has collected marine reptiles from Nevada and Wyoming.

Dr. Massare is an active member of the Society of Vertebrate Paleontology. She has taught courses on vertebrate evolution and dinosaurs at the University of Rochester, New York.